KNIGHT-DREAMS

KNIGHT-DREAMS

Broadway Empire, LLC

Knight Dreams by Nicole Elaine Avery
Copyright © 2022 NICOLE E. AVERY
First Printing, 2022
Second Printing 2023

Photography, Raffi Imaging © 2002 Velvet Series, Fabio Carli © 2005-2006 Wumon, No Cry Series
Artwork, Nicole Elaine Avery © 2002-2006

Second Edition: Added photographs and three new poems.
(Like sweetened syrup, Recess, and Restore.

ISBN: 9798985984965 (Paperback)
ISBN: 9781960826039 (Hardback)
eISBN:

First Edition: September 2022
Second Edition: April 2023, Interior updated

BE Publishing,
A division of Broadway Empire, LLC,
Bronx NY 10472
broadwaympire@gmail.com

Broadway Empire is an eclectic media company.
Printed in the United States of America

In memory of love

(An Ode to September 11th, 2001.)

A whisper heard through the rubble...

I whisper a prayer
slowly, softly... sweetly.

It crept from my heart
to the lips of my soul,
Uttered for you... my friend.

It traveled through my spirit,
Past my inner man,
To your inner ear which took delight,
While your soul smiled.

I whisper a prayer...
One full of hope,
Joy and peace.

All for you...

...A prayer I hope you, too, will
Whisper back, someday– my friend.

© Nicole Elaine Avery 2000-2023

Preamble

Knight-Dreams takes readers along a lyrical journey of love. Each stanza seamlessly synthesizes language with shifting emotions, while individual lines induce excitement, sorrow, passion, and pain… ultimately unlocking a voice once subdued, emancipating a heart robust.

Words expel onto pages from unlikely sources, such as paper napkins, parchment, or apothecary receipts until dormancy is nullified. The collection of said sources were compiled over two decades… some of which were only written in singular phrases at that given time.

Lastly, Knight-Dreams confronts break-up, painful memories and wasted love. It uncovers feelings of one-sided relationships, and the reality of defeat. While good times may have previously driven a given relationship, this book focuses its lens on hurt love and/or a love lost.

Table of Contents

First Period

The Unripened Period

Much like the residuals of eating unripened fruit, immature relationships unable to develop can leave a long-lasting taste of disgust in one's mouth.

Where has our love gone?

Where has our love gone?
One so palpable and true
Nights we'd spend with the other…
No attachments
Our hearts brimming anew.

Our friendship?
Eroded sands of time
I raise my face
It ends
With you glaring back blankly at mine.

What do I do
When one such as you is gone?
Shall I search for another?
Or settle for remnants of you?
Where else am I to find a love rhythmed in blues?

Where has our love gone?
Has it turned on itself?
Answer me!
Do you even care?
Or, have our memories to the sea been cast?

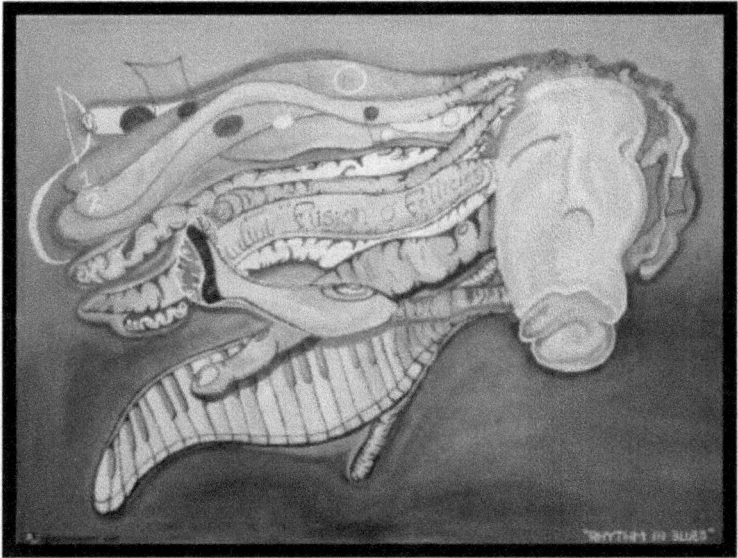

©2005. Nicole Elaine Avery. *Rhythm-in-Blues.*

How?

How does one lie
when the truth is much easier said?
An insufferable equivocation
soaring the lower empyrean.

A good friend… lost
A deceiver, gone
Along with him untold truths,
Wicked, demonstrative, songs.

Why continue this lie,
When the truth is much easier said?
May death ever favor you
thrashed about your head.

A true friend,
Mistaken for mine
I am not her,
Nor, the mother of his child,
But I know he is connected
with this cruel, mendacious, lie.

Artwork. ©2005. NEA. *Betrayal*

Heartache

Love.
Why does it hurt
like a silent auger
plunging the heart?

I'm aching!
Yes…
Love!
An incontinent splinter peripatetically traveling about one's
spine.

Love.
Why is it perverted with pain
instead of joyous favor
surrounding the soul?

Understand love?
I am without desire.
Devoid the ability
even amidst the weakest attempt.

Although
I require love,
And being held,
As does a newborn,
It is a warmth
this world
can never
offer me.

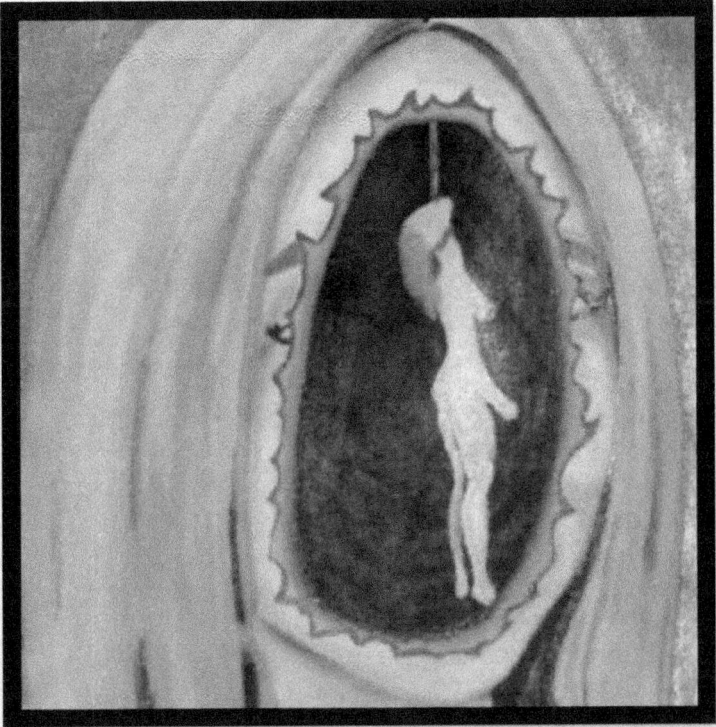

Artwork. ©2006. NEA. *Killing Me Softly.*

Delayed voice

What of life's
timekeeper
manipulating
the hands of time?

I no longer acquiesce to
backwardness.
Travel past? I resign…

How to find
the me I once knew?
With despondency,
I retreat to
bygones too few.

I seek an outlet,
Although none can I find.
I peer upon the looking glass
with wasted effort,
through a crystal mind.

Judgment

Pondering our love's innocence…
We were simply friends.
Oh, how we reverenced the other
with endless amends.

I think of you,
Envisioning all you've meant.
Relinquishing not our past,
As memories I do attend.

Who'd think the future
would align our stars
only to tear them apart?
No one can justify
this callous art!

Why the turmoil?
An outcome so easily resolved.
Amidst our strong wills,
Our love goes awry...

I yearn an alternative solution
for a love like yours.
For without you,
My soul retreats to nothingness.

Second Period

The Strawberry Period

Although this period of poems is the shortest, it represents the longest relationship sustained by the author. Ironically, she began penning her poetry towards the demise of the relationship. Acknowledging a break-up on the horizon, like many blind lovers before her, she resisted the inevitable by attempting to mend persistent holes pervading at the seams.

Have *you* ever been?

Have you ever been in a room
filled with people
and still felt alone?

Have you ever felt muted?
Distant?
Somewhere in the twilight zone?

Have you ever felt as though things would worsen?
That a change would never come?
Confused?
Listless?
Wanting someone… rejecting all?

Have you ever felt funny like you couldn't figure out
why…?
Why your life has taken this turn,
Swirling the bleak dismal sky?

Have you ever been in a room
filled with people
and still felt alone?

I have…

That's when I know it's time to go home.

Artwork. ©2006. NEA. *Illusions.*

A love lost that hasn't even begun...

I can't breathe!
My reaction to this affixation,
Ignites an attitude,
Derailing my demeanor.
It seems right... but...
To whom do I direct this fight?

This love can never be,
Because, it has never been.
Is it him, or fantasies
I've imagined?

Is it real, the way I feel?
Or, has that been misconstrued, too?

Ha, ha! I have to laugh!
I have to smile
at this twist of lies.

Why did I have to see him?
Why did he show me his smile?
Why did I have to smell him
and become familiar with his sexy style?
His walk, talk and breath.

Stop! This is insane
The way I'm carrying on...

He doesn't even know my name!
How can I be upset over a love that could never be...
When the one who dreamed everything up is me?

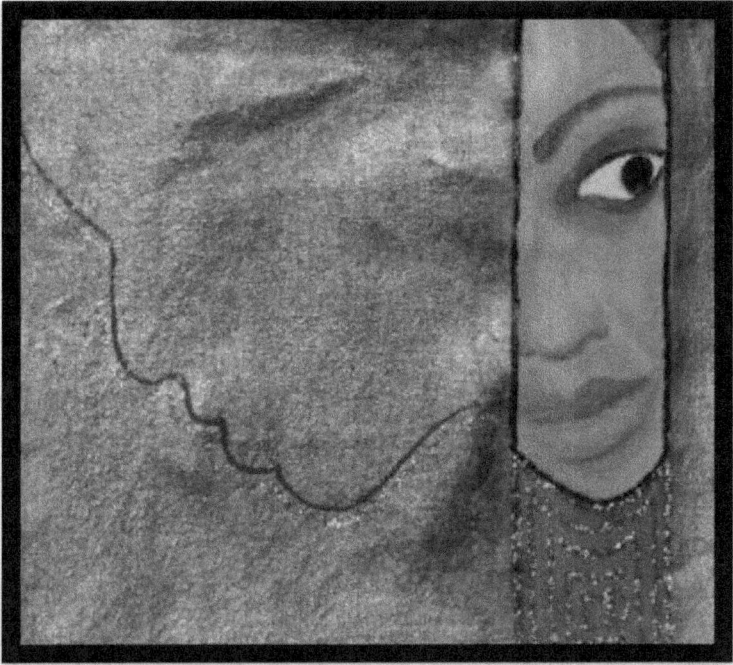

Artwork. ©2005. NEA. *Anxious.*

If not here, then where?

If this is not a place where my tears are understood,
Where do I go to cry?

If this is not a place where my spirit can take wing,
Where else do I go to fly?

If this is not a place where my questions can be asked,
Where do I go seek?

If this is not a place where my feelings can be heard,
Where do I go to speak?

If this is not a place where you can accept me as I am,
Where can I go, be?

If this is not a place where I can try and learn,
And grow,
Where can I
JUST
BE
ME?

© Nicole Elaine Avery 2000-2023

I'm misbehavin'

If I wasn't misbehavin'
Then,
I'd be saving
all my love for you!
If that were true
Then,
you'd be here.
Unfortunately,
My dear,
That isn't so!

Maybe,
it's good
you ridded yourself of me…
To live a life
free of shame and misery,
Or the pain
of having to work
at our relationship.

You had everything
handed to you
once you said, "I do!"

Yet, I refuse
to be your personal whore!

This ain't *Love Jones*
I'll learn to be alone,
Turned away from love

Well,

Right now, I'm misbehavin'
Who wants this love?
Get in line!

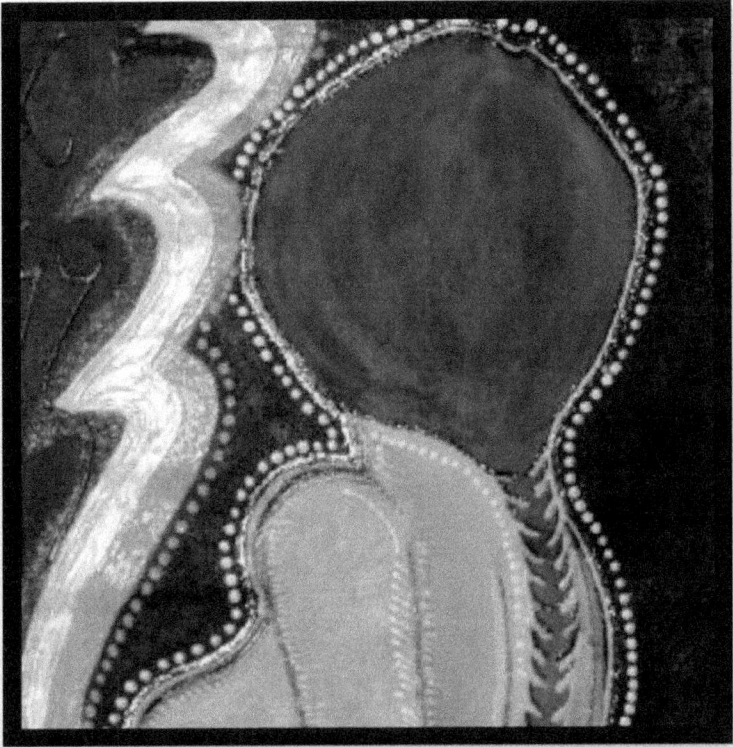

Artwork. ©2005. NEA. *I'm Not Ur Personal Whore.*

Third Period

Bruised Apple Period

Work relationships are never fun when they end. While those who are chased shield themselves with the day's schedule, the hunter falls prey to games, manipulation, and trickery. This period shares the poet's reality when mixing business with pleasure.

Mistrial

Maybe,
I should put him on trial
for a while,
And see how he feels
about what I feel.

What's the big deal, you ask?
Everyday,
he wears a mask…
While the contours of my spirit
reveal my true feelings.
I just can't adjust.
I'm finding it hard to survive this!

Flippin',
Swirling,
Skippin',
Twirling
around in my mind.
His face,
His unforgettable scent.

As predator…

Do I attack, now?
Or wait till he speaks,
Or becomes weak?

As I take-a-peek down the hall
I see his gorgeous figga'

Court is adjourned…

Lunch & learn

It's OVER!
It's finished.
The games have all been played!

Or was it me who was played?
Why is it, now,
he wants me to stay around for his antics?
Go pound for pound with his theatrics?
I've changed the lyrics in his semantics!

For, I AM TIRED!
I've retired.
It's OVER!

Artwork. ©2002. NEA. *It's Over!*

Holiday bliss

A valentine is fine,
But a husband to hold onto would be nicer.

A rose, I suppose, is what most women want...
I'd prefer a man.

Chocolates, diamonds and furs are divine,
But this time around, I want a brother who can
wine and dine me,
One I can call mine,
My very own...

Loan me your love
And I promise to give it back

Give me your love
And you won't hear no flack
Send me your love
And I'll give you exactly what you need.

Indeed
I need a man who will compliment me,
Who will love me,
And identify with me...
The things I see.

So, you see.
A valentine is fine,
But a husband to hold onto would be so much nicer.

Drip-Drop

Cry?
Why?

Drip.
Drop.

The famous sound
as they
hit the top of the floor.

Or should I hit the door running?
Or should I stay and pay the price of stupidity?

Rivers of tears
never disappear
as I continue to chase after
what is merely superficial.
Any genius recognizes
I'm not his specialty.
A facade
personifies
his feelings for me.

Invisible,
Am I.

May he suffer my distress
when I cry!
Without remorse he sees,
But does he overstand
Why?

Why I Feel emphatically weak?
My love is strongest for those who reject mine!

Empty

My heart plummets to defeat!

Downtrodden

So many he's had
as his first choice.

Rivers of tears
race the sides
of my once loving face
to the top
of an all too familiar floor.

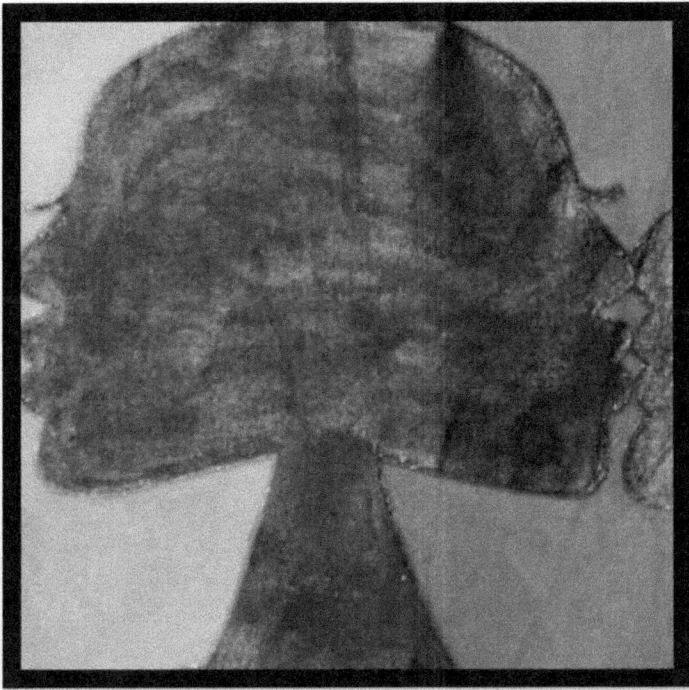

Artwork ©2006. Nicole Elaine Avery. *Confused*.

Destructive thoughts

Your love
reminds me
of a funeral
where all the women sit pretty…
Fighting for the front seat,
Fighting for first place,
For a space
in your disintegrating heart.

Why do I start falling for you?
Your charisma…
Your charm…
Can't you see
the harm you've brought me
and so many other hearts?

Why make me believe
you adored me?
Instead,
You whored me!
You've destroyed
any good thoughts
I had left of me.

© Nicole Elaine Avery 2000-2023

Artwork. ©2005. NEA. *All This Stress.*

All this stress…

Oh, My God!
All this stress I feel!
If only I peel my mind from his grip.
With all that's been said,
My heart
whirls,
then shrivels to nothingness…
And what remains?
Lies in the palm of your hand
Dormant,
At your command

Oh, Heavens, no!

This ish gotta go!
How can I feel this way
About a love that has NEVER begun?
A gun would end all this foolishness,
End the hostile behavior...
STOP!
I need a savior to guide me
Supply
All my needs
Unwind me
From
ALL
THIS
STRESS!

Artwork. ©2005. NEA. *Wumon, No Cry.*

Period Four

The Strawberry Period-Revisited

Seldomly did love dissipate, then re-appear with the same individual for the poet. This period captures the resurgence of a love lost in heart break. Within each poem, love is a journey all its own.

Absolut fantasy

I pour wine over your love
again, and again, in my mind.
Across each lifted piece of your body
I pour…

I pour it,
Quick
like honey.
Running,
Oozing,
Falling,
Flowing over each lifted piece
like paradise.

I rise,
Or…
Should I say YOU rise
to the occasion.
Sweet invasion,
Elation,
Soothing tender moans,
Oh, I'm in a zone.
Don't leave me,
You're already home,
Already there…
A pair about to explode.
Unload your love
as I continue to pour out mine.

Artwork. ©2005. NEA. *Scarlett Fantasy.*

Angel eyes

Are these angel eyes I see?
Do they truly believe in me,
Or is there some type of lie?
Conspiracy?

Are these angel eyes I see?
Is victory in my proximity?
Or is there doom and unforeseen damage and trickery
you've prepared for me?

Anger not thyself,
For this is prophecy,
What God already knew,
and He gave to me.

Thou eyes hast changed,
And so have mine.
I've been forsaken by thee
forced to roam.
I can't fathom,
why
thy eyes have changed.

They've turned cold and unbearable.
I'm left stranded by your look.
Damaged,
Yet,
Hooked.
Entangled in your fallacious webs.
Entrenched.
Enchanted, still.

Yes… your eyes destroy me,
but won't defeat me,
I must overcome.
Renounce you from
my reality.

In those eyes deception roams wild.

Untitled

Only
When
The
Eye
Loses
A
Tear

Can
It
Truly
See

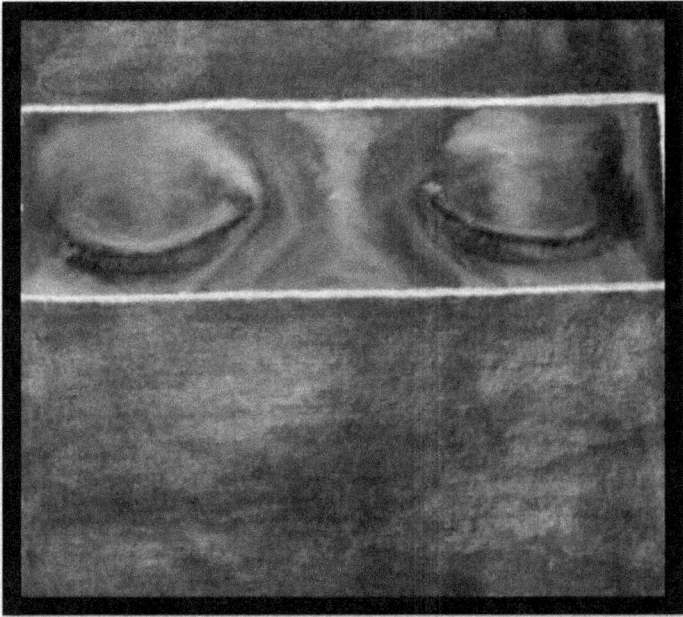

Artwork. ©2005. NEA. *Praying Eyes.*

The day after

Do you ever dream about me?
A love unforbidden?
A love whose life is incomplete without you?

Do you ever dream about me?
A dream so unforgiving?
A dream consumed with lust,
Engulfed with surreal thoughts, plaguing your soul?

Lost in a world of insecurities,
Your identity masked by terminal obscurities
Do you dream a dream about me?

Have you ever dreamed a dream about me...?
One of which you cannot tell?
Tempted by its reality,
Held back by its sensuality,
Destroyed by what you could destroy
If it were ever revealed?

Do you dream about me?
Do you?

Wouldn't you rather be with me instead of just dream?

© Nicole Elaine Avery 2000-2023

Period Five

The Mango Period

Home to the tropics, a mango is fortified with an array of vitamins and enriching elements. A ripen mango proffers that and more. The tender, juicy, stone fruit dripping with sweetened syrup can ignite pleasures unimaginable when acting as an aphrodisiac.

This period, like the others, fluctuates between strong emotions and different lovers. It also pinpoints moments that were… juicy and pleasurable.

The night spent wondering

Last night I spent wondering
Where you were.

In the arms of another?
Sharing my love with someone else?
Did you just discover that our love had faded?

Or are you merely
waiting to use me all up?

Don't stutter, my brother
Where were you?
Inside a world brand new?

Well, here's some advice
to take with you.
Understand
what a good woman is for.

Find out who you'd like to be
Then, become it
Don't let it overtake you--
If you're *the man* you claim to be.

Then,

Be strong and create a world for yourself
Don't allow the droplets of paint
To create your scenery
Without YOU.

Become the artist

Take hold
the brush

Don't rush.

Knight-Jones

Encompassed by a jungle of lox,
I peer upward,
in search of your oris.
Instead,
you about-faced me
And
I encounter love's lock.

The overwhelming passion
encapsulated my being
beyond articulation.

Entangled by your web of woven lox,
And a history of lies,
I lie paralyzed.
My mind trembling from what,
I'm not certain.
Is it what you've done to me?
Or, what you're about to do?

Don't deny me of what I've earned…
Your love.

Entranced by your hair's
puppeteering power,
I lean forward…
Thrusted backward
by some magical force.
I've become your puppet
Attached to each lock
One touch propels me to pure ecstasy.
Enfeebled by your clutch,

I surrender to my own desires...
Diving into your lustful power.

Engaged by your riveting world,
I lie motionless,
Paralytic from an open kiss
made available by you.

Engulfed completely by each worm,
I squirm,
As tiny cells of sperm
are injected.
My "perm" frizzes
as you rise,
And race higher.

Ensnared by a look you've transcended,
There's no end to the fantasy
you're fulfilling, right now.
My brow is filled with wet,
Steamy passion,
Unrationed,
Unadulterated,
Unsure...

You lure me
with your look.
You torment me with your touch.
How much more can I take?
At stake is our lives
if we were to separate right now.

Stay with me,
Encompass me,

Entangle me,
Don't deny me,
Entrance me,
Thrust backwards and forth...
Attached, I've become.
Propel me higher.
Help me to clutch my desires.
Engage me in your love
Engulf my body with yours
Make my perm fizz to a natural curl.

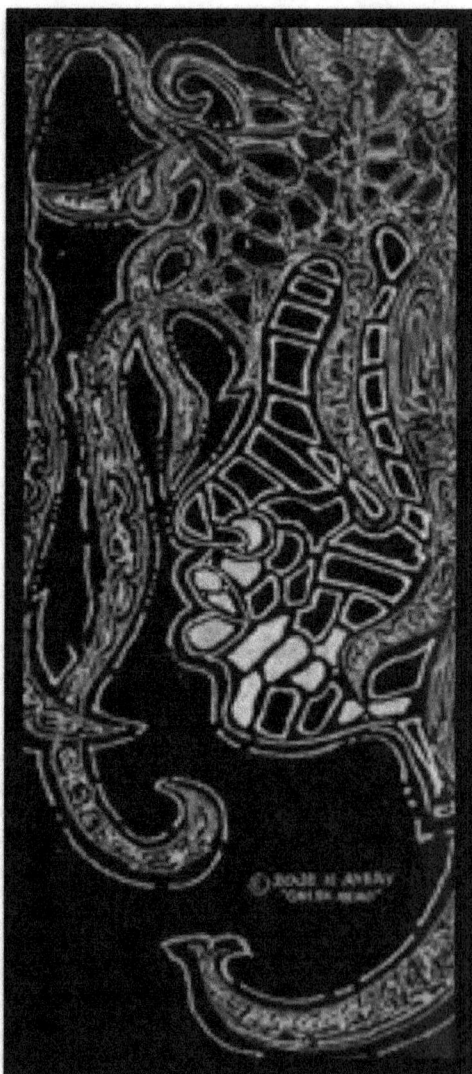

Artwork. ©2006. NEA. *Greenhead*.

Artwork. ©2002. NEA. *God's Antennae.*

Where is J-J?

I danced with you, last night…
I made love to you this morning…
Today, I write about you, uninhibitedly.

You are the background to my loving images.
My canvas was barren until I birthed your love.
You arouse in me a spirit of total inhibition,
And the agony of relentless desires.

A rushing wind swirls by me
as each thought twirls inside my mind.

You know me,
As if we met before
in a painting
where love was the brush
as well as the stroke.

Your spirit transcends me into eternity,
Before it actually begins.

You are the background to my loving images

When can our love begin?

I missed you

I missed your call, last night.
Was it that you didn't want to talk?
Or could it have been the fall
you would have taken
if your boyz had mistaken
you for being in love?
I'm sorry, lust…
As it is apparent.

Who am I kidding anyway?
You're where you are,
I'm here.

I need to see you,
Hear you,
Be with you,
Sometime soon.
I'll just wait
and see.
What will be… will be
I'm not worried.

My phone will ring.

You set my spirit free
only to abandon me.
You suggest
I live freely
As
God intended,
But you're not here
to enjoy me.

Why have you entered my life?
Making it, more, empty?

You were sent
to fill my void.
Instead
You engender
a deeper,
Darker,
Depth
In my being.

When we do speak,
You speak of such great hope
For us,
But
Are your thoughts merely fantasies?
Why'd you have to choose me?

Pruned love

You set my spirit free
My images began to
Dance to the rhythms strummed by your background

You were the reason for my smiles, my energy.
Now, the plug has been pulled
Like the lights on a Christmas tree
being packed away for next year…

My feet up,
Lying dormant
As they were before
Awaiting another brother
to come forth and take advantage of my pure love.

© Nicole Elaine Avery 2000-2023

Holidaze

It's Christmas Eve,
And you're stirring
up my spirit.

You're not even here,
And I can feel you
so near to me,
Exclusively.

While you're away
I create a madness of my own

I'll call it,
Holidaze.

© Nicole Elaine Avery 2000-2023

The death of a relationship

Last night, I shed a tear for you.

Yes,
One tear.

I wish you knew the measure
of my feelings.
If only you could venture
beyond this teardrop
to the brown eye adoring you.

You were my tears' salvation,
Now, you simply birth them in me.

Night after night...
I turn over to touch you,
I reach out and your frame
I no longer feel.
I suffer greatly.
My life, a disorder without you

My dreams imbue empty thoughts
Your voice
Resounds...
Bellowing...
Endlessly,
Taunting my soul.

Tonight, I shed a tear for you.
For me.
This is my only hope
to cope without having you near,

I fear that for you and I
Our love has died.

Artwork. ©2006. NEA. *Tear Drop.*

Period Six

Fruit Cocktail Period

(with light syrup)

The fruit cocktail period hosts individuals of one rhythm. Some of the words serve merely as fantastical fantasies, while for others, the words function in revelatory bliss.

Lightly sweetened syrup

Your love,
Linguistically,
Oozes down my proverbial spine,
Lightly, like sweetened syrup

Like lyrics to a soulful song

You string me along,
And…

I HATE IT!

Can't stop it from dragging me deeper.
I seek help
To only feel weaker

Remorse
Entranced

I can't stop, but don't want to

I want chu,
Yes. you.

Only.
Teardrops.
Fall.

© Nicole Elaine Avery2000-2023

This love

May the fruit of my love
bloom within your being...
A conception of purity.

As the wind blesses, and blows,
The seasons change.
May our love for one another remain
Un-wavered,
Weathering the storms
to come.

Growing, well-rooted...
A relationship standing firm.

In time,
may we find
more love,
Joy,
Peace,
Together…
Bonded by truths.

My hope?
Our hearts ripen
to a deeper consciousness,
Filling each strand with
the knowledge of understanding,
Forbearing anything that would attempt in
breaking this bond

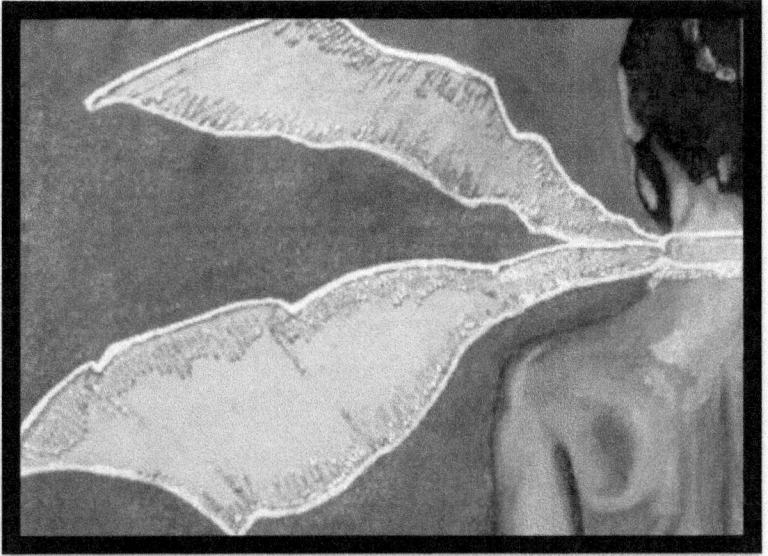

Artwork. ©2006.NEA. *Awareness*.

That's not me!

Afraid to smother the other,
So…
In deep cover
we remain.

This is, yet, strange
Since you're so outward
about everything else.

My heart melts
when I see you.
My tastebuds swell
when they feel you
up close and personally.

But what about the public view?
It's then that I wonder…
Who am I to you?
And
Everyone else?

A clown?
Some chick
growing
old with wait?
Someone to fondle your fever?

Well, that's not me.

Mood swing

I swing.
You swing
from one feeling to the other...
Next day, to another.

I'm exhausted from the shifting,
The wishing
I was yours...
Yours truly.

Who's to say why we're here?
Why we've met?
And yet,
You still refuse
to try.

You swing left,
I swing right.
In flight
we both change the other 's mind
time and again.
Who wins?

There are no winners.

We both lose
We lose each other.

Footprints of the heart

Last night, you left a footprint in my spirit
A blueprint of love.
My spirit drawn to your spirit.

Dust particles,
Remnants,
And prints.

You've given me a reassurance
Of whom I am,
Of what I've become...
A piece of your world,
A participant in your thoughts.
A rhythm to the beat of your breaths
You've left footprints of love on my life
Your prints force me towards the world
I couldn't bear without them.

© Nicole Elaine Avery 2000-2023

For now…

For now,
I will hold you.
For now,
I will touch you,
And evade your thoughts.

Sublime…

For now,
Your love is mine.
So, I will merely hold on,
For now…

When I'd ask about our status
your answer would always be…
For now.

You never did foresee our love being forever
It
Was
Always,
Simply...
For now.

© Nicole Elaine Avery 2000-2023

The challenge is yours…

While I struggle to find myself and you guide me
to restoration…

What have I given you?
You've been my protector
What have I given you?
You've been my laughter
What have I given you?
You've brought life to a listless soul.

Love is what I feel,
But how do I relay this to you
Without watching you walk
and witness my world wither away?

You are my breath…
My air…
You've become my life,
My heart needs to stay.

It's all a game…

If you were a poker player,
I would be your full house…
Packed with all the things a man desires.

I'd provide you with a life
unlike any other.

I'd make you drop the phone
and think of no one
but me.

The night you called,
I started to hang up…
Intending to incite a ruckus.
Get you excited,
Leave you there…
Physically unsatisfied.
…As I 've been
for months on end.

Yet, I did not.

That night you called
I hoped another would call, too.
Overshadowing you.

Still, I lie here in wait

Lit

As the candle burns,
I yearn for your love.
I yearn for your touch,
Your trust...
Caress me.

I reach towards your reach.
I fear what is about to transpire.
My heart blazons
as every inch of you draws nigh.

Repeatedly,
I imagine your love…
How deeply it will transcend.
I release the thought
while letting you in…
Endlessly.

As the candle burns,
I yearn for you.
I yearn for your love…
And all your body can do to mine.

My flame remains lit for you
As I sit here with you
Honoring you as you honor me.

Artwork. ©2006. NEA. *Mystical Baby.*

Con Wiche

He is the *Adobo*
en mi fried curry chicken…
The salsa y merengue
en mi hip-hop and R&B!
La Boriqua de mi pasado.
A love
I once knew,
but shouldn't…
Esta bien!
At least,
I knew a love, anyway.

Artwork. ©2006. NEA. *Wiche.*

FREEdoM

For years
I had fears
about jumpin into sumthin
new
with you.

You put yourself out there.
Our connection was real,
Like our kiss on the corna'

If I could freeze that moment in time,
we'd be together, right now
Instead of me sitting here
writing

I love deliberately
And struggle with letting go,

But once you fell back
I had to set you free,
Give you over to freedom.

Artwork ©2006. NEA. *Para-dice Lost.*

Rewind

You remind me so much of myself,
A day when I was happy.
I know that you were placed in my life
to bring that back…
Restore who I once was…
The life I was beginning to capture…

I love you.

The person on the inside,
The things you represent,
And, yet,
I don't even know much about you.
Yes, you're real,
But who are you?

I must be the rib missing from your side
separated by a garden of misconception,
Deception,
Lies,
Reprise…
Why?

I want that life back!
I want it, now!

Artwork. ©2006. NEA. *Betrayal*.

Recess!

The door closes
Yet love never really ends.
It's sent searching

It bends
It turns
Until …

Love abounds.
Rebounds
Taught to fend.

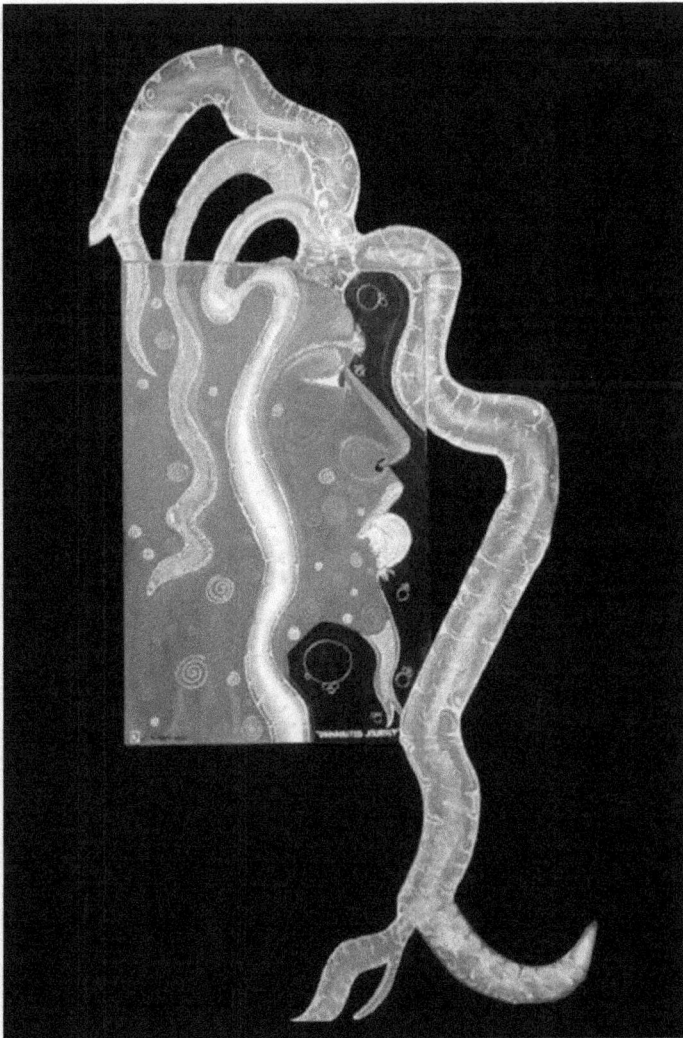

Artwork. ©2002. NEA. *Uninhibited Journey*.

Restore

Restore us
Mend us, before us,
Right before our eyes

Our lips
Our thighs

All need cleansing
Not compromise

Our insides
Where our thoughts reside

Arise,
and take hold
of my soul

Cleanse me,
Clean
I lean on You,
I glean through

This immense pain

Restore us
You bore us
Now, burden my shame.

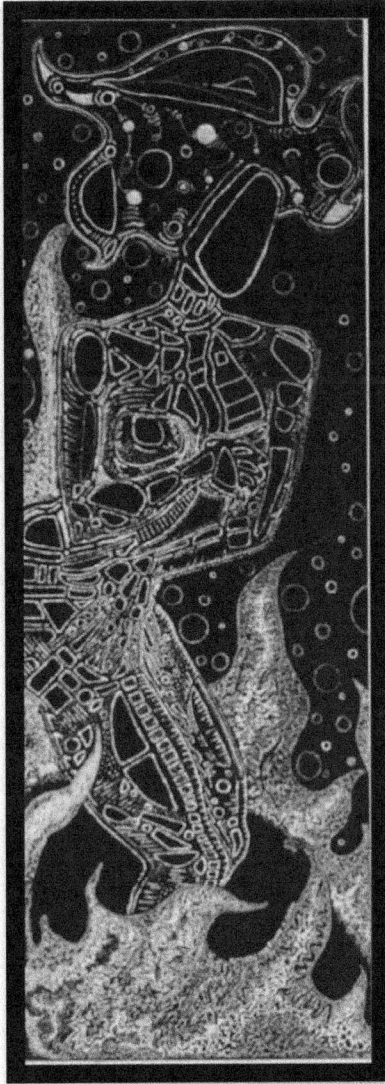

Artwork. ©2006. NEA. *Refiner's Fire*.

Thank you for your purchase!

Dr. Avery's books are available on Amazon.com, Goodreads.com, Googleplay.com, BN.com, and through Readersfavorite.com

The next three pages include other books written by the author. More titles are forthcoming. Be sure to follow the author on Amazon.com.

Send requests for art prints to broadwaympire@gmail.com

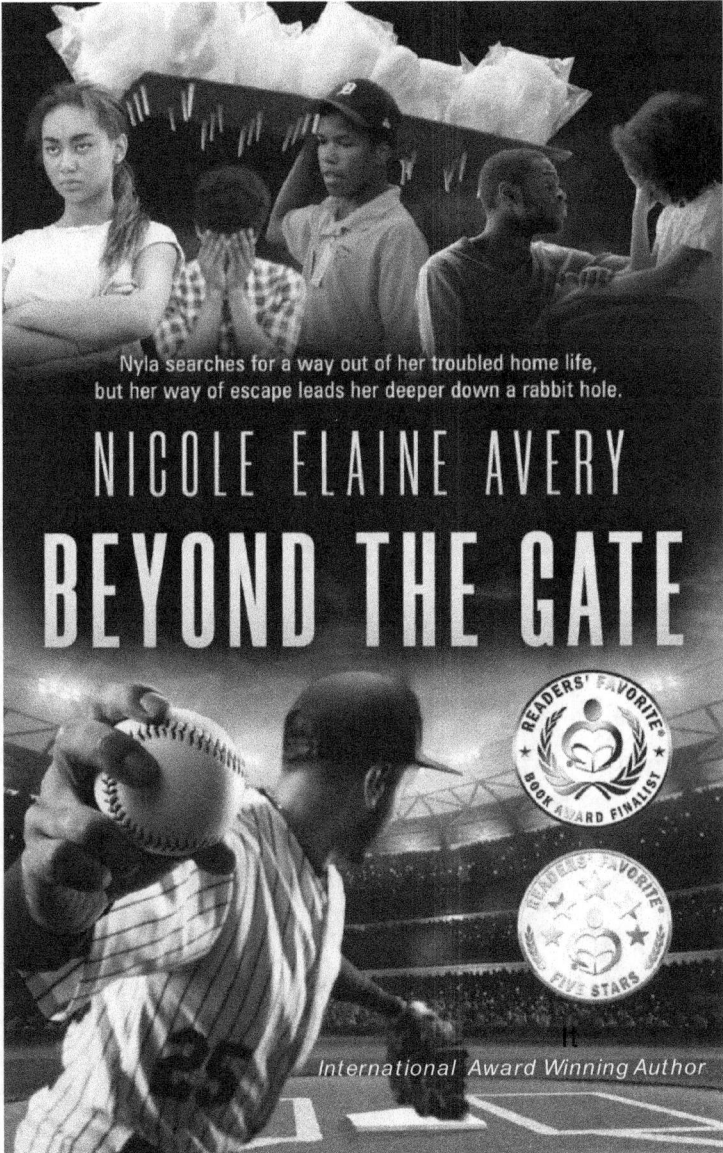

Nyla searches for a way out of her troubled home life,
but her way of escape leads her deeper down a rabbit hole.

NICOLE ELAINE AVERY

BEYOND THE GATE

READERS' FAVORITE
BOOK AWARD FINALIST

READERS' FAVORITE
FIVE STARS

International Award Winning Author

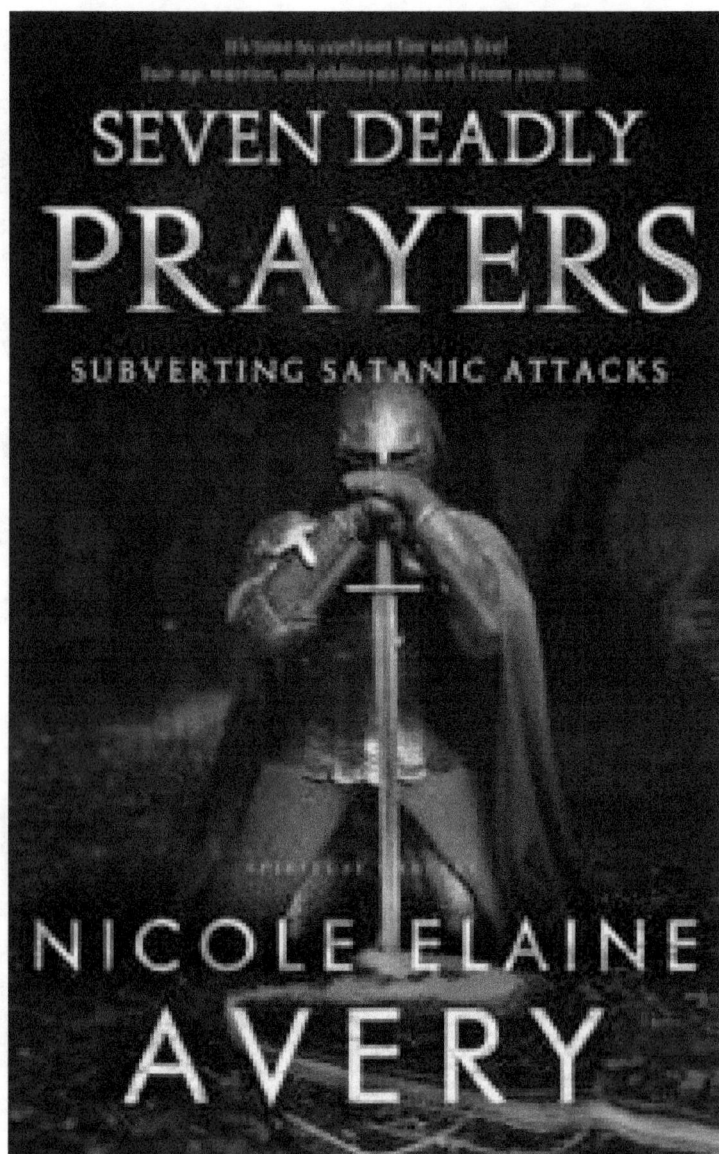

It's time to confront fire with fire!
Suit up, warrior, and obliterate the evil from your life.

SEVEN DEADLY
PRAYERS

SUBVERTING SATANIC ATTACKS

NICOLE ELAINE
AVERY

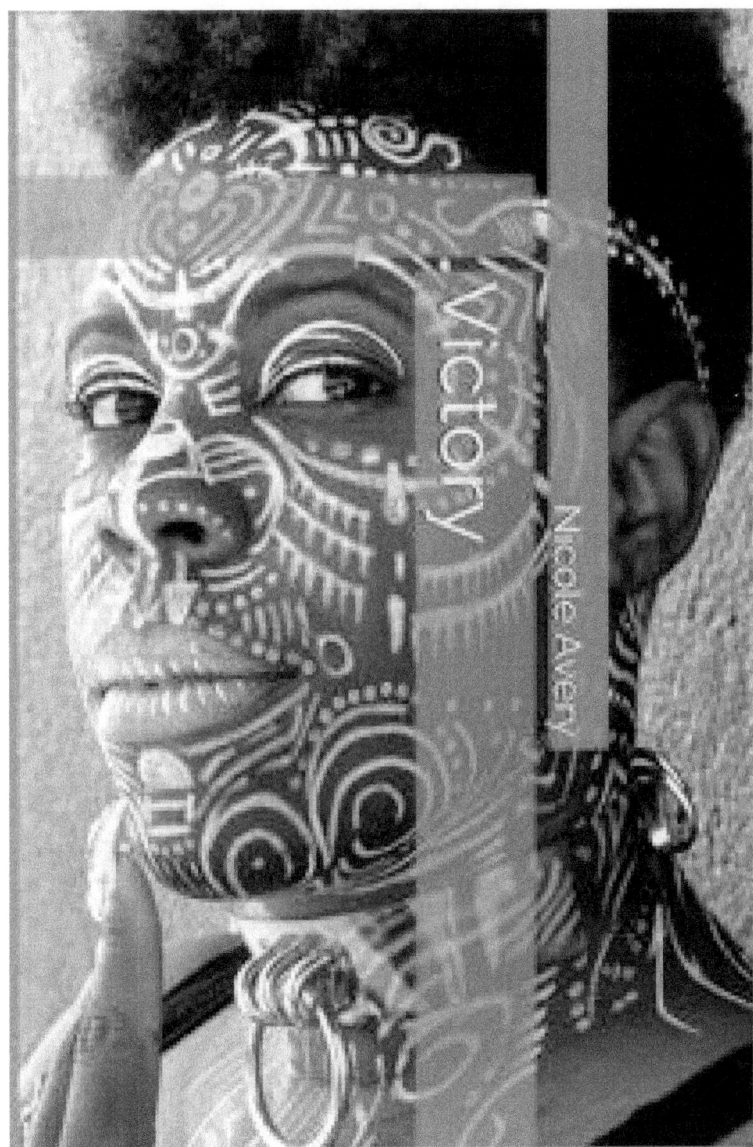

Victory

Nicole Avery

Notes

Notes

_____
_____
_____
_____
_____
_____
_____
_____
_____
_____
_____
_____
_____
_____
_____
_____
_____
_____
_____
_____
_____
_____
_____
_____
_____
_____

www.ingramcontent.com/pod-product-compliance
Lightning Source LLC
LaVergne TN
LVHW021540080426
835509LV00019B/2750